Temba Munsaka

Organizational Theory: The importance of Stakeholders in Project Management

GRIN Verlag

Bibliografische Information der Deutschen Nationalbibliothek:

Die Deutsche Bibliothek verzeichnet diese Publikation in der Deutschen National-
bibliografie; detaillierte bibliografische Daten sind im Internet über http://dnb.d-
nb.de/ abrufbar.

Imprint:

Copyright © 2013 GRIN Verlag GmbH
Druck und Bindung: Books on Demand GmbH, Norderstedt Germany
ISBN: 978-3-656-55328-1

TEMBA MUNSAKA

Organizational Theory:

Discuss the importance of Stakeholders in project management citing relevant examples

Program: Doctorate of Project Management

ATLANTIC INTERNATIONAL UNIVERSITY

Table of Contents

Introduction

Contemporary project management recognizes the importance of stakeholder involvement in project initiation, planning and execution. This is particularly so as stakeholder's interests, involvement and expectations all influence project execution as well as its impact. Project management is the planning, organizing, directing and controlling of resources for a relatively short-term objective that has been established to complete specific goals and objectives[1]. Stakeholders refers to any individuals, groups, or institutions who have a vested interest in the natural resources of the project area and who potentially will be affected by project activities and have something to gain or lose if conditions change or stay the same[2]. Thus in the context of project management, stakeholders are all those who need to be considered in achieving project goals and whose participation and support are crucial to its success. Stakeholders can be internal to the project or external. The major stakeholders in project management are the project managers, project team, sponsors of the project, customers or project beneficiaries, government, local communities among others. In project management, stakeholders are identified through stakeholder analysis. Stakeholder analysis identifies all primary and secondary stakeholders who have a vested interest in the issues with which the project or policy is concerned[3]. The main aims of stakeholder analysis are to identify the interests of stakeholders and potential areas of conflict as well as ways to reduce negative impacts on vulnerable and disadvantaged groups[4]. The importance of stakeholders is in project management is evident at different levels. Firstly, it gives the concerned people say over how projects may affect their lives. Secondly, it is essential for project sustainability. Thirdly, it generates a sense of ownership if initiated early in the development process. Fourthly, it builds capacity and enhances responsibility. Fifthly, it provides opportunities for learning for both the project team and stakeholders themselves. This paper thus examines the importance of stakeholders in project management informed by the view that all the important decisions during initiation, planning and execution stages of the project are made by these stakeholders.

---

[1] Kerzner, H, 2011:11.
[2] Boonstra, A 2006:38–52
[3] Golder, B and Gawler, M 2005:2
[4] Mitchell, R.K., Agle B.R. & Wood, D.J,1997: 83-86

Key Terms

Project- A project is a temporary structure to organize and manage work and ultimately to build a specific defined deliverable or set of deliverables[5]

Project team- The project team consists of the full-time and part-time resources assigned to work on the deliverables of the project. They are responsible for understanding the work to be completed; completing assigned work within the budget, timeline, and quality expectations; informing the project manager of issues, scope changes, and risk and quality concerns; and proactively communicating status and managing expectations.[6]

Constraints- Constraints are limitations that are outside the control of the project team and need to be managed around[7]

Critical path- The critical path is the sequence of activities that must be completed on schedule for the entire project to be completed on schedule[8]

Stakeholders- Stakeholders are anyone who has an interest in the project. Project stakeholders are individuals and organizations that are actively involved in the project, or whose interests may be affected as a result of project execution or project completion[9]

Milestone- A milestone is a scheduling event that signifies the completion of a major deliverable or a set of related deliverables[10]

Key stakeholders considered in project management

It is essential from the outset to highlight the fact that, the high failure rate of major projects has been attributed to a lack of attention to stakeholders. Negative attitudes of stakeholders towards a project can cause cost overruns and time schedule delays due to conflicts over project design and implementation[11]. With this in mind it is practically necessary at this juncture to define key project stakeholders as a build up to the discussion of the importance of stakeholders in project management. The key stakeholders in projects are the sponsors. Project sponsors or owners are the people who pay for the project[12]. In developing countries

---

[5] http://www.techrepublic.com/article/mini-glossary-project-management-terms-you-should-know/6109067
[6] Ibid
[7] http://www.techrepublic.com/article/mini-glossary-project-management-terms-you-should-know/6109067
[8] Ibid
[9] http://en.wikipedia.org/wiki/Project_stakeholder
[10] http://www.techrepublic.com/article/mini-glossary-project-management-terms-you-should-know/6109067
[11] WWF. 2000:3.
[12] Cleland, D, I. 1986: 36.

4

such as Zimbabwe, project sponsors are usually foreign donors and they normally set the goals and standards for the projects. Failure to meet or observe the standards set by the donors has affected the implementation of certain projects in Zimbabwe. For example in the past decade 2000 to 2010 most projects in Zimbabwe have collapsed or failed to take off the ground as a result of disagreements with the donors. Projects such as the dualisation of major highway routes such as the dualisation of the Harare –Beit Bridge road have moved at a snail's pace as they have failed to attract sponsors or donors as the government is at variance with the conditions that prospective sponsors are putting in place.

Project managers are also key stakeholders who are responsible for the planning, leading, organizing and control of project activities as well as personnel to achieve project objectives[13]. In fact project managers are the ones primarily responsible for identifying and building synergies with all other relevant stakeholders. Effective project managers are those who identify all the relevant stakeholders that can contribute to the success of a project. This can only be possible if the project managers make a comprehensive stakeholder analysis. It must be reiterated that, the goal of stakeholder analysis is to develop a strategic view of the human and institutional landscape, and the relationships between the different stakeholders and the issues they care about most.

Apart from the project managers another important stakeholder are the project teams. A project team refers to the personnel employed in the project, who carry out specialized activities within the project to achieve set objectives[14]. It is crucial that the project team should work collectively so that the project goals and schedules are attained within the specified time frame. Project teams come from diverse cultural, social, economic and political backgrounds. The challenge therefore for project managers is to mould a project team that is bound by a shared vision, organizational culture and common purpose. A coherent project team is better placed to cooperate with other relevant project stakeholders increasing the chances of achieving the project objectives.

Project customers or beneficiaries are also important stakeholders. Simply stated, project customers or beneficiaries are people or groups who buy the product and obtain the benefit from the project's outcomes[15]. Thus for any project to succeed, it has to be sensitive to the needs and demands of the project beneficiaries. In recent times the general public has

---

[13] Legris, P. & Collerette, P. 2006:64-76.
[14] Kerzner, H. 2012: 11.
[15] Kerzner, H ,2012:12.

become an important stakeholder in project management. Public stakeholders therefore are people who are concerned about the project's environmental, social or economical impacts, such as the media[16]. Suppliers are part of the stakeholders as they provide goods and services used by the project. The perceptions of public stakeholders can influence a project in terms of whether it succeeds or fails to achieve its set objectives. If the public particularly views a project as desirable for society that project is often painted in positive light[17]. For example the circumcision project has received positive media coverage as it is seen as a part of the broad effort to curb HIV prevalence among the adult population in Zimbabwe. The roping in of notable entertainment icons such as the popular Winky D has increased the appeal of the circumcision project to the general public. This has seen women also welcoming and encouraging their male partners to get circumcised. Thus this shows that the stakeholder approach which targets the target beneficiaries can be enhanced if the general public and the media are also incorporated.

Thus projects that succeed tend to be those that consider the interests and strike a balance between the demands of diverse stakeholders. Often, project stakeholders hold different views with respect to a given project, it is therefore up to the project managers to take into consideration these different views and factor them into the initiation, planning and execution phases of projects[18]. This increases the chances of project success. The only way the interests of the stakeholders can be identified and understood is through a thorough stakeholder analysis. In this regard project managers must be proactive when it comes to identifying relevant stakeholders. For instance in project management there is sometimes need to trade-off the needs of one stakeholder against another. This is only possible if the relevant stakeholders to a project are properly identified and their interests known. Stakeholder participation in project management is made through avenues such as consultations, dialogues, partnerships, workshops and conferences[19].

Importance of stakeholders in project management

As already alluded stakeholder participation in project initiation, planning, implementation is key to project success. Stakeholder participation is visible at all the stages of the project cycle. In fact the project cycle holds that any project worth the name project should ensure that it enhances value for stakeholders. This clearly shows that stakeholders are of great

---

[16] Ibid p 13.
[17] Ibid p 14.
[18] Turner, J. R.,2009:5.
[19] WWF. 2000:3

importance in any project. The importance of stakeholders in project management is shown by the following:

Gives people say on how projects may affect their lives

Stakeholder participation is of central importance in project management as it allows people to voice their concern on how projects may affect their lives[20]. Projects do not occur in a vacuum; they are initiated and implemented within a given social, economic, political, technological and environmental context. As a result projects have an impact on different aspects of peoples' lives. Given that projects impact on peoples' lives it is therefore imperative for the same people to be afforded a voice at the initiation, planning and execution of projects.

The most important stakeholder that should be given greater say on how projects may affect their lives are the target beneficiaries[21]. More often project initiators and implementers ignore the project beneficiaries or tend to be paternalistic by unilaterally deciding for them certain projects. The result is usually projects that are divorced from the needs and interests of the beneficiaries. For example in developing countries such as Zimbabwe, the target beneficiaries are not given greater say on how developmental projects may affect their lives. Way back in the 1950s the Tonga people were not given an opportunity to voice their concern on how the Kariba dam project was to impact on their lives. The net effect was that by the time Kariba dam was completed Tonga communities which had lived side by side since time immemorial found themselves alienated by imposed borders. In a broad sense the Tonga social fabric was torn apart irreparable even up to this day. If the Tonga allowed to voice their concerns on the Kariba dam project maybe measures would have been put in place to remove trans-movement restrictions such as passports and visas if they wanted to visit their kin either side of the Zambezi River.

The importance of stakeholders was visible during the implementation of the Communal Areas Management Programme for Indigenous Resources (CAMPFIRE) programme and its downstream projects in Zimbabwe in the 1980s[22]. Local communities as well as the target beneficiaries were given an opportunity to voice their concern on how the project was going to affect their lives. This helped the government, donors and other relevant stakeholders to plan the project in a way that was to benefit the target communities and the animals which

---

[20] WWF, 2005:2
[21] Ibid p 3.
[22] WWF, 2005:4

7

were to be the source of benefit. Thus at implementation CAMPFIRE met with minimum resistance from the target communities as their concerns were factored into the project before it was implemented.

In a broad sense it is critical for the project management team to allow all relevant stakeholders to voice their concerns on how projects may affect their lives. This reduces potential conflicts that may jeopardize the whole project initiative. Furthermore, the importance of allowing stakeholders to voice their concern on how the project will impact on their lives allows buy ins. In the context of project management stakeholder buy in refers to support that the stakeholders render to a project so that it can be successful in meeting its objectives.

It is this writer's concern that in most cases from practicability, the communities under which the projects are implemented have no say in what happens in the project decision making. The people that fund the projects have the greater say on how to run things at the detriment of other stakeholders.

Generating a sense of project ownership

The importance of stakeholders in project management also lies in the fact that allowing stakeholder participation generates a sense of project ownership[23]. Project ownership is a key variable that has a bearing on the success or failure of projects. In the majority of cases projects that succeed are those in which a sense of ownership is engendered in all relevant stakeholders. This starts at the initiation phase where there are wide consultations with all relevant stakeholders. At the initiation phase of the project, consultations are meant to give all relevant stakeholders a chance to voice their concerns on how the proposed project will affect their lives and also give the project team an opportunity to interact with target beneficiaries[24]. Above all, the consultations are usually aimed at generating a sense of ownership in all the relevant stakeholders particularly the target beneficiaries. In the CAMPFIRE projects there were wide consultations with the target communities. By telling the target communities that they were the true beneficiaries of the projects, these communities developed a sense of ownership of the CAMPFIRE programme and its related projects.

Instilling a sense of ownership in the relevant stakeholders is also critical at the planning and implementation as well as the evaluation phases of projects. At all the aforementioned

---

[23] WWF-UK. 2000:3.
[24] Ward, S.; Chapman, C, 2008: 563–577.

phases all relevant stakeholders are suppose to give their input which in most cases may make or break the project. If there is a deep sense of ownership of the project it is most likely that the relevant stakeholders will give supports that will make the project a success. This strategy was effectively used by Practical Action an international nongovernmental organization operating in Zimbabwe for the development of its mini hydro power station projects in the Manicaland province[25]. Practical Action first instilled a sense of ownership in the target communities and also enlisted the support of the government as a way of giving the project official legitimacy. Once the target beneficiaries saw that the government was involved it was easy for them to assume ownership of the hydro power projects. The target communities are now actively involved in the maintenance of the hydro power stations as they strongly feel that they have an ownership stake in these power stations.

However, projects such as irrigation schemes given to people in Masvingo particularly the Nyatare irrigation project in the Zaka district have collapsed as a result of lack of ownership by the relevant stakeholders such as the target beneficiaries[26]. The irrigation project was initiated with minimum consultation with all the relevant stakeholders. As a result the project never instilled a sense of ownership in the target beneficiaries and community. The government and the donors were seen as the owners of the project. Thus the maintenance of the project was left to the government and donors instead of the target beneficiaries. Eventually, with time the project collapsed as it was not clear on who really owned the project. This shows that engaging all relevant stakeholders is important in project management as it clarifies ownership of projects.

Engagement with relevant stakeholders helps to build and generate a sense of ownership that is needed if a project is to be successfully planned and executed. This is particularly desirable in developing countries such as Zimbabwe, where most projects are donor or government initiated with little or no ownership at all by the important stakeholder, the target beneficiaries or communities.

This author believes that ownership without proper capacity impartation and training will not make sense as the beneficiaries in most cases have no technical know how to manage and sustain the projects.

---

[25] *Practical Action* '2011:10.
[26] Sunday Mail September 2011

Building Capacity and Responsibility

The importance of stakeholders in project management is that it allows for the building of capacity and responsibility for projects. In the context of project management capacity building refers to strategies or measures put in place to enhance the efficiency, effectiveness and responsiveness of projects to the needs of the target beneficiaries. Capacity building is usually at different levels[27]. The first critical level is that of human resources. Projects need to be implemented and maintained by people with the requisite skills and knowledge. Thus by engaging all relevant stakeholders, skills and knowledge can be collectively developed that can make the project a success. For example in poultry projects vets can be hired to train the target beneficiaries on how to look after the chickens until they reach maturity. Target beneficiaries can also be taught on how to market the chickens once they reach maturity. With this form of capacitation greater benefit can be derived from projects.

Capacity building can also be done through training on resource mobilization and management. Resource mobilization includes all the activities aimed at raising resources for a project and how these resources are managed. Projects that succeed are usually those in which relevant stakeholders are able to mobilize both material and financial resources. It is needless to point out that projects entail the commitment and utilization of material and financial resources to achieve project objectives. Project teams and target beneficiaries thus need to be capacitated with the skills to mobilize and manage these resources in such a way that project objectives are achieved at minimum cost. This thus requires training in financial management in areas such as budgeting, bookkeeping and auditing.

Stakeholder engagement also promotes responsibility for the project. Project responsibility denotes sense of duty, care and support that is given to a project so that it achieves its set objectives[28]. Usually projects that achieve their objectives are those where there is a high sense of responsibility among all the relevant stakeholders at initiation, planning and execution. Project responsibility can be developed and engendered through wide consultation, dialogue and building partnerships among the key stakeholders. For example the European Union, in Zimbabwe, has tried to cultivate a sense of responsibility for its sponsored projects in the areas of health and nutrition. Target beneficiaries, are encouraged to be responsible for projects such as nutritional gardens. This has seen these projects surviving well after the EU have left.

---

[27] Wood, D. J and Gray, B. 1991:136-162.
[28] Schwager, H. P. 2004:35

This writer believes that whilst on paper, the above point makes sense and yet in reality it may be difficult as the community will need to have the basic education to understand the technical architecture of the project. And the fact that the project may have been imposed on the communities in which case they will never adopt it as theirs fully.

Ensuring Project Sustainability

The importance of stakeholders in project management lies in ensuring project sustainability. Project sustainability refers to the ability of the project to meet the current needs as well as the capacity to do so in the foreseeable future long after the donors have left[29]. In developing countries such as Zimbabwe, the issue of project sustainability is a burning one. Often projects collapse once target beneficiaries are left on their own. This suggests lack of sustainability measures. Project sustainability can thus be attained if there is stakeholder participation. Stakeholder participation in projects allows for all relevant stakeholders to devise measures that ensure projects are sustainable. If there is dialogue and wide consultations with relevant stakeholders it is likely that solutions can be developed to ensure that projects are sustainable. For example World Vision and CARE International in Zimbabwe have tried to build sustainability in their projects by encouraging widespread stakeholder participation in their nutritional gardens projects. Project Sustainability has been increased by allowing other players such as the government through the Agricultural Extension Services department (AREX) to come on board and support the target beneficiaries with agricultural knowledge on what crops to grow and when to grow them. Thus project sustainability is only achievable if there is the engagement of all the relevant stakeholders.

Provides learning opportunities for both the project team and stakeholders

The importance of stakeholder participation in project management is that it provides for a learning opportunity for both the project team and stakeholders themselves[30]. Projects as once off activities generate valuable lessons which have to be learnt by both the project teams and the relevant stakeholders. From these lessons ways can be generated to improve future projects if the initial model is replicated elsewhere[31]. When the project teams and relevant stakeholders engage they can share notes on the positive and negative aspects associated with the initiation, planning and execution of certain projects. This is why most projects sponsored by donors such as support for people living with HIV and AIDS in Zimbabwe, bring relevant

---

[29] Bourne, L. and Weaver, P, 2010:12.
[30] Levinson, J. C., Smith, M. S. A., & Wilson, O. R, 1999
[31] Levinson, J. C., Smith, M. S. A., & Wilson, O. R, 1999

stakeholders together to review progress made hitherto and identify challenges that could have limited progress towards the achievement of set objectives. The essence of these all stakeholder meetings is to derive lessons from the projects being implemented. These lessons help in promoting the sustainability of projects, engendering a sense of project ownership and project responsibility among all the relevant stakeholders.

That said, the author feels that especially in Zimbabwe, the political orientation of the funder and indeed the project management team plays a critical role in motivating learning opportunities. A properly planned project will fail to impart the required knowledge simply because the funder is perceived to be biased towards a particular political philosophy.

Reduces negative impact on vulnerable groups

Reducing the negative impact on vulnerable groups is another area where the importance of stakeholders can be seen in project management. Vulnerable groups are those people who stand to lose or be negatively affected by the implementation of a given project[32]. The identification of the vulnerable groups is only possible through stakeholder engagement. When all the relevant stakeholders are engaged their submissions can indicate the people who are likely to suffer if a given project is adopted and implemented[33]. Once the vulnerable groups are properly identified through stakeholder participation measures can be put in place to mitigate the negative impact of the project. In the Marange area engagement with relevant stakeholders has enabled the diamond mining companies, such as Anjin, to generate measures to assist people to be affected by their mining operations. Some of the measures include relocations to build areas as well as compensation for their lost ancestral homes. Though the level of compensation has generated a lot of controversy in Marange among the human rights based organizations the most important lesson derived is that stakeholder participation helps vulnerable groups to be treated fairly if they are negatively affected by projects.

Enables identification of potential areas of conflict

Stakeholder participation in project management is important as it helps project managers to identify areas of potential conflict that may negatively affect the project[34]. In the implementation of projects it is inevitable that there are areas of potential conflict. It could be on who benefits from the project, who implements the project, who regulates the project as well as who chooses the project alternative to be implemented. To avoid or minimize

---

[32] Ibid p5.
[33] Chinyio, E. A. & Akintoye, A. 2008:591-599
[34] Crowther, D,2008:47-63.

conflicts associated with projects it is imperative that all relevant stakeholders should be consulted. Through consultations and dialogue with relevant stakeholders project managers are able to identify all areas that have the potential to be sources of conflicts when the project is being implemented. All stakeholder meetings among other purposes also serve the purpose of identifying areas that can be sources of conflict. Once potential areas of conflict associated with a project are identified it is easier to develop mitigation measures before the envisaged conflicts arise.

Conclusion

There is no denying that in contemporary project management stakeholders are of paramount importance. Projects that achieve their objectives are those that take into account the interests of all the relevant stakeholders. Stakeholder participation is evident at the initiation, planning and implementation of projects. Thus project managers need to carry out a comprehensive stakeholders analysis that identifies different stakeholders and their vested interests. This increases the chances of project success.

References

Boonstra, (2006) A Interpreting an ERP-implementation project from a stakeholder perspective *International Journal of Project Management* 24

Bourne, L. & Weaver, P. (2010)' Mapping stakeholders'. *In Construction stakeholder management.* (eds. Chinyio, E.A. & Olomolaiye, P.). Malaysia, Wiley-Blackwell

Chinyio, E. A. & Akintoye, A. (2008) 'Practical approaches for engaging stakeholders: findings from the UK'. *Construction Management and Economics*, 26(6)

Cleland, D, I.(1986) Project Stakeholder Management. *Project Management Journal*, 17(4)

Crowther, D. (2008) Stakeholder perspectives on social responsibility. In D. Crowther and N. Capaldi (Eds.), (2008) *The Ashgate Research Companion to Corporate Social Responsibility,* Aldershot: Ashgate Publishing

Golder, B and Gawler, M *Cross(2005) -Cutting Tool Stakeholder Analysis,* London WWF

Kerzner, H.(2011) *Project-Based Metrics, KPIs and Dashboards* , London, John Wiley & Sons

Kerzner, H. (2012) 'Project Managers's Understanding of Stakeholders's Satisfaction' in Project Perspectives London International Project Management Association

Legris, P. & Collerette, P.(2006) Roadmap for it project implementation: integrating stakeholders and change. *Project Management Journal*; 37(5)

Mitchell, R.K., Agle B.R. & Wood, D.J. (1997) Toward a theory of stakeholder identifi cation and salience: defi ning the principle of who and what really counts. *Academy of Management Review.* 22(4)

Practical Action (2011) 'Mini Hydro Power Stations' London Practical Action

Sunday Mail September (2011). Zimpapers Publication-Zimbabwe

Schwager, H. P. (2004). *Organizational strategies to address stakeholder relationships : A customer perspective portal* PhD thesis Aubum University

Turner, J. R. (2009) *The Handbook of Project Based Management: Leading Strategic Change in Organizations,* New York, McGraw-Hill

Ward, S and Chapman, C.(2008)' Stakeholders and uncertainty management in projects', *Construction Management and Eco- nomics* 26(6)

Wood, D. J.; Gray, B. (1991) 'Toward a comprehensive theory of Collaboration' *Journal of Behavioural Science* 27 (2),p 136-162.

WWF.(2000) *Stakeholder Collaboration: Building Bridges for Conservation.* Washington, DC WWF Ecoregion Conservation Strategies Unit, WWF US

WWF-UK. Partnership Toolbox. WWF-UK, Surrey, United Kingdom. Accessed from: htps://intranet.panda.org/documents/document.cfm?uFolderID=51380&uDocID=51065 on 15 August , 2013.